C000135141

THE SIGN OF FOUR

AN AQA ESSAY WRITING GUIDE

MIRANDA MATTHEWS

First published in 2021 by Accolade Tuition Ltd
71-75 Shelton Street
Covent Garden, London WC2H 9JQ
www.accoladetuition.com
info@accoladetuition.com

Copyright © 2021 by Miranda Matthews

The right of Miranda Matthews to be identified as the author of this work has
been asserted by her in accordance with the Copyright, Designs and Patents Act
1988.

All rights reserved. No part of this book may be reproduced in any form or by
any electronic or mechanical means, including information storage and retrieval
systems, without written permission from the author, except for the use of brief
quotations in a book review.

Image, Page x ('Sir Arthur Conan Doyle - Statue') Copyright © Summoned by
Fells. Licensed under CC BY 2.0: https://creativecommons.org/licenses/
by/2.0/legalcode.
Source: https://www.flickr.com/photos/summonedbyfells/15208530123

Image, Page xii ('Contemplation') Copyright © Mike Knell. Licensed under
CC BY-SA 2.0: https://creativecommons.org/licenses/by-sa/2.0/legalcode.
Source: https://www.flickr.com/photos/mpk/3543169767

Image, Page 9 ('221 Baker Street') Copyright © Luca Melloni. Licensed under
CC BY-SA 2.0.
Source: https://www.flickr.com/photos/lmello85/6389006409/

Image, Page 42 ('where is watson?') Copyright © Nikos Roussos. Licensed
under CC BY-SA 2.0.
Source: https://www.flickr.com/photos/comzeradd/4265857576/

ISBN 978-1-913988-17-3

FIRST EDITION
1 3 5 7 9 10 8 6 4 2

CONTENTS

Editor's Foreword   v

Essay Plan One   1
Essay Plan Two   10
Essay Plan Three   20
Essay Plan Four   28
Essay Plan Five   36
Essay Plan Six   44
Essay Plan Seven   53

Endnotes   61
Accolade Press for GCSE English: The Range   63

EDITOR'S FOREWORD

In your GCSE English Literature exam, you will be presented with an extract from Arthur Conan Doyle's *The Sign of Four* and a question that asks you to offer both a close analysis of the extract plus a commentary of the novella as a whole. Of course, there are many methods one *might* use to tackle this style of question. However, there is one particular technique which, due to its sophistication, most readily allows students to unlock the highest marks: namely, **the thematic method**.

To be clear, this study guide is *not* intended to walk you through the novel scene-by-scene: there are many great guides out there that do just that. No, this guide, by sifting through a series of mock exam questions, will demonstrate *how* to organise a response thematically and thus write a stellar essay: a skill we believe no other study guide adequately covers!

I have encountered students who have structured their essays all sorts of ways: some by writing about the extract line by line, others by identifying various language techniques and giving each its own paragraph. The method I'm advocating, on the other hand, involves picking out three to four themes that will allow you to holistically answer the question: these three to four themes will become the three to four content paragraphs of your essay, cushioned between a brief introduction and conclusion. Ideally, these themes will follow from one to the next to create a flowing argument. Within each of these thematic paragraphs, you can then ensure you are jumping through the mark scheme's hoops.

So to break things down further, each thematic paragraph will include various point-scoring components. In each paragraph, you will quote from the extract, offer analyses of these quotes, then discuss how the specific language techniques you have identified illustrate the theme you're discussing. In each paragraph, you will also discuss how other parts of the novel further illustrate the theme (or even complicate it). And in each, you will comment on the era in which the novel was written and how that helps to understand the chosen theme.

Don't worry if this all feels daunting. Throughout this guide, Miranda (the author!) will be illustrating in great detail – by means of examples – how to build an essay of this kind.

The Conan Doylean equivalent of a selfie.

The beauty of the thematic approach is that, once you have your themes, you suddenly have a direction and a trajectory, and this makes essay writing a whole lot easier. However, it must also be noted that extracting themes in the first place is something students often find tricky. I have come across many candidates who understand the extract and the novel inside out; but when they are presented with a question under exam conditions, and the pressure kicks in, they find it tough to break their response down into themes. The fact of the matter is: the process is a *creative* one and the best themes require a bit of imagination.

In this guide, Miranda shall take seven different exam-style questions, coupled with extracts from the novel, and put together a plan for each – a plan that illustrates in detail how we will be satisfying the mark scheme's criteria. Please do keep in mind that, when operating under timed conditions, your plans will necessarily be less detailed than those that appear in this volume.

Now, you might be asking whether three or four themes is best. The truth is, you should do whatever you feel most comfortable with: the examiner is looking for an original, creative answer, and not sitting there counting the themes. So if you think you are quick enough to cover four, then great. However, if you would rather do three to make sure you do each theme justice, that's also fine. I sometimes suggest that my student pick four themes, but make the fourth one smaller – sort of like an afterthought, or an observation that turns things on their head. That way, if they feel they won't have time to explore this fourth theme in its own right, they can always give it a quick mention in the conclusion instead.

IN MEMORY OF
SIR ARTHUR CONAN DOYLE
BORN ON 22 MAY 1859 CLOSE TO THIS SPOT
DONATED TO THE CITY OF EDINBURGH BY
EDINBURGH AND LOTHIANS BRANCH OF THE FEDERATION OF MASTER BUILDERS
ON THE FEDERATION'S 50ᵀᴴ ANNIVERSARY
UNVEILED ON 24 JUNE 1991 BY
PROFESSOR GEOFFREY D. CHISHOLM
ChM, PRCS.Ed,FRCS.Eng,FRCP Ed, F.R.A.C.S(Hon),F.C.S(SA)(Hon)
President, The Royal College of Surgeons, Edinburgh

A plaque in Edinburgh — nearby Conan Doyle's birthplace.
Copyright © Summoned By Fells

Before I hand you over to Miranda, I believe it to be worth-
while to run through the four Assessment Objectives the exam
board want you to cover in your response – if only to demonstrate how effective the thematic response can be. I would
argue that the first Assessment Objective (AO1) – the one that
wants candidates to 'read, understand and respond to texts' and
which is worth 12 of the total 34 marks up for grabs – will be
wholly satisfied by selecting strong themes, then fleshing them
out with quotes. Indeed, when it comes to identifying the top-
scoring candidates for AO1, the mark scheme explicitly tells
examiners to look for a 'critical, exploratory, conceptualised
response' that makes 'judicious use of precise references' – the
word 'concept' is a synonym of theme, and 'judicious refer-

ences' simply refers to quotes that appropriately support the theme you've chosen.

The second Assessment Objective (AO2) – which is also responsible for 12 marks – asks students to 'analyse the language, form and structure used by a writer to create meanings and effects, using relevant subject terminology where appropriate.' As noted, you will already be quoting from the novella as you back up your themes, and it is a natural progression to then analyse the language techniques used. In fact, this is far more effective than simply observing language techniques (personification here, alliteration there), because by discussing how the language techniques relate to and shape the theme, you will also be demonstrating how the writer 'create[s] meanings and effects.'

Now, in my experience, language analysis is the most important element of AO2 – perhaps 8 of the 12 marks will go towards language analysis. You will also notice, however, that AO2 asks students to comment on 'form and structure.' Again, the thematic approach has your back – because though simply jamming in a point on form or structure will feel jarring, when you bring these points up while discussing a theme, as a means to further a thematic argument, you will again organically be discussing the way it 'create[s] meanings and effects.'

AO3 requires you to 'show understanding of the relationships between texts and the contexts in which they were written' and is responsible for a more modest 6 marks in total. These are easy enough to weave into a thematic argument; indeed, the theme gives the student a chance to bring up context in a relevant and fitting way. After all, you don't want it to look like you've just shoehorned a contextual factoid into the mix.

Finally, you have AO4 – known also as "spelling and grammar." There are four marks up for grabs here. Truth be told, this guide is not geared towards AO4. My advice? Make sure you are reading plenty of books and articles, because the more you read, the better your spelling and grammar will be. Also, before the exam, perhaps make a list of words you struggle to spell but often find yourself using in essays, and commit them to memory.

A statue of Sherlock Holmes in Meiringen, Switzerland. Copyright © Mike Knell.

My (and Miranda's!) hope is that this book, by demonstrating how to tease out themes from an extract, will help you feel more confident in doing so yourself. I believe it is also worth mentioning that the themes that have been picked out in the course of this guide are by no means definitive. Asked the very same question, someone else may pick out different themes, and write an answer that is just as good (if not better!). Obviously, the exam is not likely to be fun – my memory of them is pretty much the exact opposite. But still, this is one of the very few chances that you will get at GCSE level to actually be creative. And to my mind at least, that was always more enjoyable – if *enjoyable* is the right word – than simply demonstrating that I had memorised loads of facts.

ESSAY PLAN ONE

This extract comes near the beginning of the novel, as Holmes discusses his detective work with Watson before the adventure begins.

"The work itself, the pleasure of finding a field for my peculiar powers, is my highest reward. But you have yourself had some experience of my methods of work in the Jefferson Hope case."

"Yes, indeed," said I, cordially. "I was never so struck by anything in my life. I even embodied it in a small brochure with the somewhat fantastic title of 'A Study in Scarlet.'"

He shook his head sadly. "I glanced over it," said he. "Honestly, I cannot congratulate you upon it. Detection is, or ought to be, an exact science, and should be treated in the same cold and unemotional manner. You have attempted to tinge it with romanticism, which produces much the same effect as if you worked a love-story or an elopement into the fifth proposition of Euclid."

"But the romance was there," I remonstrated. "I could not tamper with the facts."

"Some facts should be suppressed, or at least a just sense of proportion should be observed in treating them. The only point in the case which deserved mention was the curious analytical reasoning from effects to causes by which I succeeded in unravelling it."

I was annoyed at this criticism of a work which had been specially designed to please him. I confess, too, that I was irritated by the egotism which seemed to demand that every line of my pamphlet should be devoted to his own special doings. More than once during the years that I had lived with him in Baker Street I had observed that a small vanity underlay my companion's quiet and didactic manner. I made no remark, however, but sat nursing my wounded leg. I had a Jezail bullet through it some time before, and, though it did not prevent me from walking, it ached wearily at every change of the weather.

Starting with this extract, examine how Conan Doyle portrays Holmes and Watson as contrasting characters in *The Sign of Four*.

Write about:

• **How Conan Doyle portrays Holmes and Watson at this moment in the novel.**

• **How Conan Doyle portrays Holmes and
Watson in the novel as a whole.**

Introduction

I often suggest kicking off the introduction with a piece of
historical or literary context, because this ensures you are
scoring AO3 marks (marks that too often get neglected!) right
off the bat. It's then a good idea to quickly touch on the themes
you are planning to discuss, since this will alert the examiner to
the fact that AO1 is also front and centre in your mind.

'Given the cultural cross-currents that swept through
the Victorian era – the raw emotions from the earlier
Romantic era on the one hand; the increasing bent
towards scientific empiricism on the other – it is
perhaps unsurprising that Conan Doyle injected some
of these tensions into his sleuthing duo.[1] Watson is the
more sentimental and imaginative of the two, whereas
Holmes is drier and more pragmatic. This dichotomy is
explored in this extract as the two men proffer
competing interpretations of Watson's 'A Study In
Scarlet'; however, notably, their shared interest in
authorship also hints at points of convergence in their
personalities.'[2]

Theme Paragraph One: Conan Doyle portrays Watson in this passage as sensitive to criticism and easily hurt by his friend's dismissal of his

literary efforts. Holmes, contrarily, appears oblivious to any pain he may have caused Watson.

- The most obvious contrast between the two friends here is the emotional gulf that seems to sit between them. Holmes' criticism of Watson's work cuts the latter deeply, and although he attempts to remonstrate: 'But the romance was there...', Holmes quickly adds to his own argument without considering the effect his rejection of Watson's work might have on his devoted friend.[3] Holmes appears to be unemotional himself, but also unable to comprehend and give support to the emotions of others. [*AO1 for advancing the argument with a judiciously selected quote; AO2 for the close analysis of the language*].

- Conan Doyle adds to the poignancy of the criticism by breaking the fourth wall in a literary context – since the author's first Sherlock Holmes novel was the discussed *A Study in Scarlet*, purportedly by Watson, any reader who enjoyed it might be amused or disgruntled to find out from the hero himself that they should not have done so.[4] When Watson admits his book was 'specially designed to please Holmes' the reader may feel pity for him; at no stage in the novel does Holmes do anything 'specially designed to please' anyone else, and arguably he would never think to do so. [*AO1 for advancing the argument with a judiciously selected quote; AO2 for the close analysis of the language*].

- <u>Elsewhere in the novel</u>: Watson is hurt again at the end of the final chapter of the novel, when he tells Holmes of his engagement to Mary Morstan. Holmes gives a 'most dismal groan' and responds, as in the excerpt above, 'I really cannot congratulate you'. A reaction like that to such a meaningful announcement from a close friend could be considered shockingly upsetting; and the comment is given extra emphasis through its placement in the novel's final paragraphs. However, by now the reader is arguably used to Holmes' habitual brusqueness and might not be surprised by his words.[5] [*AO1 for advancing the argument with a judiciously selected quote; AO2 for the close analysis of the language and for discussing how structure shapes meaning*].

Theme Paragraph Two: Sherlock Holmes and Dr Watson are given different physiques to emphasise their contrasting characters, and their occasional opposing views give their conversations throughout the book a dramatic tension, providing a foil to each other in an established literary tradition.

- When a literary character has a foil, it serves to highlight and differentiate the personalities of the two creations. Even their different physical characteristics are often delineated, which can work as a metaphor for their separate views: Shakespeare's Falstaff and Prince Hal in the Henry IV plays and Cervantes' Don Quixote and Sancho Panza are two famous examples of this literary trope. [*AO3 for placing the text in literary context*].
- Holmes is described by Conan Doyle (and thus

Watson) in *A Study In Scarlet* as 'Over six
feet...excessively lean...' with '...sharp and piercing
eyes...' and 'a thin hawk-like nose'. Watson, in other
Sherlock Holmes stories, is variously described as
strongly built, of average stature, with a thick neck
and a moustache. [*AO1 for advancing the argument
with a judiciously selected quote*].

- However, the focus on Watson's bullet wound in this
extract is used to more directly juxtapose the two
men's physical states. The very fact that Watson
needs to clarify that the wound 'did not prevent [him]
from walking' implies a degree of severity: this wound
is serious enough that Watson needs to reassure us of
his mobility. While it is true that when Watson is
called to be active by Holmes, Watson (or, indeed,
Conan Doyle) often appears to forget this disability,
its existence nevertheless crystallises a physical gulf
between the men, which is arguably a metaphor for
their divergent personalities and approaches. [*AO1
for advancing the argument with a judiciously selected
quote; AO2 for the close analysis of the language*].

- Indeed, in this very extract one can see the dramatic
tension that arises from their diverging personalities,
which is arguably more intriguing for the reader than
if Watson was simply a "Yes man" to his extraordinary
friend. Perhaps though, the reader identifies much
more easily with Watson, as he is not only the narrator
whose eyes we see through, but depicted as an
"ordinary" man who feels the usual human emotions.

**Theme Paragraph Three: Conan Doyle appears to
sometimes endow Holmes and Watson with**

similar characteristics, and gives them interests in common. It could be argued that if they had nothing that they shared, in personality or interests, they would hardly work well as a team.

- From this extract and the rest of the first chapter, the reader can see that one interest Holmes and Watson have in common is authorship; they are both writers, despite one being a detective and the other a medical doctor. A few paragraphs after this passage Holmes describes himself as being '...guilty of several monographs'. Their style and methods are very different, as is made clear, but nevertheless they both have published their writings. Watson admits that the title of his brochure, *A Study In Scarlet*, is 'somewhat fantastic', so one can presume he wanted to place the adventure in an exciting light to attract readers, much as Conan Doyle might have done himself. [*AO1 for advancing the argument with a judiciously selected quote*].

- It is notable that a 'small vanity', of which Holmes is accused by Watson, might be something else the two have in common, since Watson is so piqued by Holmes' lack of enthusiasm for his writing that he turns to nursing his wounded leg, a possible metaphor for the wound Holmes has dealt to his pride.[6] The two heroes of the novel might prove to be a little more similar in character than they appear on the surface. [*AO1 for advancing the argument with a judiciously selected quote; AO2 for the close analysis of the language*].

- Elsewhere in the novel: Watson and Holmes share the

same horror of moral depravity, as the reader can see when Jonathan Small describes the murder of the merchant Achmet to the detectives. Watson is appalled, and observes Holmes and Jones, who 'had the same disgust written upon their faces'. The reader can infer a close similarity in their ethical judgement. [*AO1 for advancing the argument with a judiciously selected quote; AO2 for the close analysis of the language*].

Conclusion

There are all sorts of options available to us when we write a conclusion. My view is that, however you decide to tackle the conclusion, you want to try and say something new: leave the examiner on a high. On this occasion, I've picked up any AO3 marks going spare by bringing in literary context, and used this as a springboard to wrap things up.

'In *The Club of Queer Trades* – a collection of short-stories, written by Conan Doyle's contemporary, G. K. Chesterton – the judge, Rupert Grant, is a brilliant detective, and stands in contrast to the less intuitive narrator, Charlie Swinburne. Both Swinburne and Watson function as conduits through which the reader might be organically informed of a brilliant detective's thought processes and methods – in other words, Conan Doyle presents the gulf between his duo as a necessary narrative mechanism. Yet for all their differences, there are also similarities between Holmes and Watson, which are arguably the bedrock of their friendship. Holmes, for instance, displays a

Watsonesque empathy when Thaddeus Sholto happens across his brother's corpse: Holmes comforts him ('You have no reason for fear') and 'kindly' pats his shoulder.'

A plaque paying homage to Sherlock Holmes in Baker Street, London. Copyright © Luca Melloni

A t this point in the novel, Sherlock Holmes has just begun to investigate the murder of Bartholomew Sholto, when the police arrive at Pondicherry Lodge.

"Here's a business!" he cried, in a muffled, husky voice. "Here's a pretty business! But who are all these? Why, the house seems to be as full as a rabbit-warren!"

"I think you must recollect me, Mr. Athelney Jones," said Holmes, quietly.

"Why, of course I do!" he wheezed. "It's Mr. Sherlock Holmes, the theorist. Remember you! I'll never forget how you lectured us all on causes and inferences and effects in the Bishopgate jewel case. It's true you set us on the right track; but you'll own now that it was more by good luck than good guidance."

"It was a piece of very simple reasoning."

"Oh, come, now, come! Never be ashamed to own up. But what is all this? Bad business! Bad business! Stern facts here,—no room for theories. How lucky that I happened to be out at Norwood over another case! I was at the station when the message arrived. What d'you think the man died of?"

"Oh, this is hardly a case for me to theorise over," said Holmes, dryly.

"No, no. Still, we can't deny that you hit the nail on the head sometimes. Dear me! Door locked, I understand. Jewels worth half a million missing. How was the window?"

"Fastened; but there are steps on the sill."

"Well, well, if it was fastened the steps could have nothing to do with the matter. That's common sense. Man might have died in a fit; but then the jewels are missing. Ha! I have a theory. These flashes come upon me at times.—Just step outside, sergeant, and you, Mr. Sholto. Your friend can remain. —What do you think of this, Holmes? Sholto was, on his own confession, with his brother last night. The brother died in a fit, on which Sholto walked off with the treasure. How's that?"

"On which the dead man very considerately got up and locked the door on the inside."

Starting with this extract, explore how Conan Doyle depicts the relationship between Holmes and the police in *The Sign of Four*.

Write about:

• **How Conan Doyle depicts the relationship between Holmes and the police at this moment in the novel.**

• **How Conan Doyle depicts the relationship between Holmes and the police in the novel as a whole.**

This time, instead of focusing in on general historical trends, my introduction is discussing instead the literary context surrounding Conan Doyle's work, and this is another way of securing AO3 (context) marks. Once again, though, you'll notice how I shift from remarks designed to satisfy AO3 criteria to remarks that nod to the themes I intend to discuss.

'The police force and their forebears have long been the objects of satire in literature: one need look no further than Shakespeare's Dogberry and Elbow for a case in point. In what is considered the first modern detective story, 'The Murders in The Rue Morgue', Edgar Allen Poe's detective, M. Dupin, is able to solve the crime when the official police are completely baffled, and the less than competent authorities are resentful of Dupin's superior powers much as Athelney Jones is scathing of Holmes' methods in this passage. However, Holmes appears to be surprisingly indulgent of the police force in *The Sign Of Four* and he seems happy to include them in his adventures when he has need of their resources to finally lay hands on the criminal. That said, he consistently uses dry humour to gently mock their inefficiency.'

Theme Paragraph One: In this extract Conan Doyle uses derogatory physical descriptions of Athelney Jones to belittle him in the reader's eyes, whilst emphasising Holmes' condescending attitude to him and the police in general.

- This excerpt introduces Athelney Jones to the reader, and immediately some details of the relationship between Holmes and the police are revealed. The officer's poor physical attributes can arguably be seen as a metaphor for his intellectual insufficiency; just before the passage begins he is described as 'very stout...red-faced...puffy'. When he addresses Holmes he wheezes, in a 'muffled, husky voice'. He is characterised as being over-emphatic – in this one passage his speech is studded with eleven exclamation marks – in marked contrast to Holmes, who answers him in simple one-sentence responses and speaks 'quietly' and 'drily' as if to calm the policeman's excitable rants. [*AO1 for advancing the argument with a judiciously selected quote; AO2 for the close analysis of the language and for discussing how form and structure shapes meaning*].

- We might agree with Thaddeus Sholto when he says later 'There is nothing more unaesthetic than a policeman'.[1] The first impressions of how the official and unofficial detectives will work together do not appear auspicious from this early extract. [*AO1 for advancing the argument with a judiciously selected quote*].

- Elsewhere in the novel: Later in this chapter, despite

Holmes' obviously superior powers of observation and deduction, he does concede to Watson that Jones 'has occasional glimmers of reason'. Given Holmes' capacity for understatement and dislike of hyperbole, this could be considered almost as praise of the policeman.[2] [*AO1 for advancing the argument with a judiciously selected quote; AO2 for the close analysis of the language*].

Theme Paragraph Two: Jones is given some of the same characteristics as Holmes by Conan Doyle – vanity and arrogance – and they both seem unaware of their own faults. Unlike Holmes, though, Jones is portrayed as having no cause to be pleased with himself.

- Conan Doyle can be said to set up a relationship between Holmes and Jones where both parties have great faith in their own abilities and believe themselves the superior detective. Thus Athelney Jones speaks patronisingly to Holmes, saying the latter's solving of a case was 'more by good luck than good guidance' and, even more comically, grandly allows that: 'Still, we can't deny that you hit the nail on the head sometime'. This is one of the several clichés that Jones uses throughout the book, his homespun "wisdom" emphasising the difference between himself and Holmes, who does not employ those manners of speech. Holmes can respond by teasing Jones with dry humour: 'This is hardly a case for me to theorise over', when he knows Jones secretly craves his input. [*AO1 for advancing the argument*

*with a judiciously selected quote; AO2 for the close
analysis of the language].*

- However, the difference is that Holmes is fully aware
  of the policeman's misplaced condescension, whereas
  Holmes' irony passes over the head of Athelney Jones.
  Elsewhere in the novel: After the capture of Jonathan
  Small, Jones comes into the boat cabin where Holmes,
  Watson and Small sit, and announces 'Quite a family
  party...I think we may all congratulate each other'.
  Conan Doyle has Jones assume as much credit for the
  successful detection as Holmes, although all Jones has
  done before the final capture is arrest several people,
  all but one of whom are completely innocent. The
  effect is absurd, especially when he then accuses
  Holmes of '...cutting it rather fine'. *[AO1 for
  advancing the argument with a judiciously selected
  quote; AO2 for close analysis of the language].*

**Theme Paragraph Three: The police are presented
by Doyle as desperately needing Holmes' help
with their investigations, whereas Holmes has no
need of them for his detection methods except
when he needs official manpower.**

- There is a power imbalance in Holmes' relationship
  with the police in this excerpt (Holmes' quick
  understanding of the situation contrasting strongly
  with Jones' blustering alliteration: 'Bad business! Bad
  business!') and in *The Sign of Four* as a whole, as is
  traditional in the Holmes stories and detective fiction
  in general. Here Holmes is not called in by the police,
  as he is on occasion by Inspector Lestrade in other

adventures; but it is clear that Jones looks to Holmes for ideas and guidance, however much he affects to belittle Holmes' achievements.[3] When, in this extract, Jones explains his own unlikely theory to Holmes, he ends it by asking 'How's that?' in a blatant and rather pitiable attempt to get Holmes' advice or approval. *[AO1 for advancing the argument with a judiciously selected quote; AO2 for the close analysis of the language]*.

- Sherlock Holmes himself is happy to use police help when he needs to, as one individual cannot count on the resources a whole force can muster, and the relationship between him and Jones is good enough for him to invite Jones to dinner later in the book. Holmes seems to enjoy his company, as Jones 'proved to be a sociable soul in his hours of relaxation'. *[AO1 for advancing the argument with a judiciously selected quote]*.

Theme Paragraph Four: Conan Doyle could depict the police as venal and corrupt, and have Holmes despise and avoid them, but he appears to use their relationship with Holmes for some light comic relief within the plot.

- At the end of the 1870s, a decade before Conan Doyle wrote *The Sign Of Four*, three out of the four chief inspectors of London's Detective Branch were found guilty of corruption, which prompted a clearing out of old hierarchies and the formation of the first C.I.D. Conan Doyle could have easily presented the Metropolitan police as venal and malfeasant.

However, in this passage and in the novel in general, the author arguably decides to bring some light relief to a story full of theft and murder by using Holmes' relationship with the police as an opportunity for comedy. [*AO3 for invoking relevant historical context*].

- The absence of self-knowledge shown by Jones in this passage, where at one moment he is deriding Holmes for theorising: 'Stern facts here – no room for theories' and at the next moment producing ludicrous theories of his own as to Bartholomew Sholto's death, is comic irony; Holmes' response 'On which the dead man very considerately got up and locked the door on the inside' is comically sarcastic. [*AO1 for advancing the argument with a judiciously selected quote; AO2 for the close analysis of the language*].

- <u>Elsewhere in the novel</u>: At the end of the adventure, despite the loss of the treasure meaning there will be no percentage reward for Jones, he is still able to produce humour of a kind when he says to Small that he 'will take particular care that you don't club me with your wooden leg' as he takes him to prison. Jones and Holmes share a sense of humour, although it could be argued that the former's is rather broad and obvious, whilst Holmes' wit is drier and more subtle – as befits their disparate characters. [*AO1 for advancing the argument with a judiciously selected quote*].

Conclusion

Again, notice that my conclusion does not simply try to sum up; rather, it tries to add something new in a way that gestures towards the mark scheme's criteria. On this occasion, I am seeking to pick up any AO3 marks going spare by bringing in relevant historical information.

'Less than a decade after writing *The Sign Of Four*, Conan Doyle became involved in two closed police cases himself, where he believed people had been falsely accused and imprisoned. He was successful in getting both cases reopened, and it could be extrapolated that he himself had a cynical view of the police force. However, Athelney Jones has his likeable qualities, and Holmes' attitude towards him and other policemen seems tolerant and even kindly. Holmes never seems to want official recognition for his part in bringing criminals to justice; as Watson remarks at the novel's close, 'Jones gets the credit', which gives the reader another reason to understand why the police encourage Holmes' involvement in a case.'

An illustration from Richard Gutschmidt depicting Holmes, Watson and Miss Marston as they hear the story of Thaddeus Sholto.

This passage in the novel comes at a point when Holmes and Watson, using the dog Toby's sense of smell, are following the trail of Jonathan Small on foot through London.

———

We had during this time been following the guidance of Toby down the half-rural villa-lined roads which led to the metropolis. Now, however, we were beginning to come among continuous streets, where labourers and dockmen were already astir, and slatternly women were taking down shutters and brushing door-steps. At the square-topped corner public houses business was just beginning, and rough-looking men were emerging, rubbing their sleeves across their beards after their morning wet. Strange dogs sauntered up and stared wonder-ingly at us as we passed, but our inimitable Toby looked neither to the right nor to the left, but trotted onwards with his nose to the ground and an occasional eager whine which spoke of a hot scent.

We had traversed Streatham, Brixton, Camberwell, and now found ourselves in Kennington Lane, having borne away through the side-streets to the east of the Oval. The men whom we pursued seemed to have taken a curiously zigzag road, with the idea probably of escaping observation. They had never kept to the main road if a parallel side-street would serve their turn. At the foot of Kennington Lane they had edged away to the left through Bond Street and Miles Street. Where the latter street turns into Knight's Place, Toby ceased to advance, but began to run backwards and forwards with one ear cocked and the other drooping, the very picture of canine indecision. Then he waddled round in circles, looking up to us from time to time, as if to ask for sympathy in his embarrassment.

"What the deuce is the matter with the dog?" growled Holmes. "They surely would not take a cab, or go off in a balloon."

"Perhaps they stood here for some time," I suggested.

"Ah! it's all right. He's off again," said my companion, in a tone of relief.

Starting with this extract, explore how Conan Doyle makes use of London as a background to *The Sign of Four*.

Write about:

• How Conan Doyle makes use of London as a background at this moment in the novel.

• How Conan Doyle makes use of London as a background in the novel as a whole.

Introduction

Notice here how I invoke both the more broad-brush historical context of London and the more focused historical context related to Conan Doyle's life. Admittedly, I'm showing off a little bit, and hitting just one of these would likely hit the AO3 criteria. That said, you can get away with pushing the boat out on occasion.

'In the second half of the nineteenth century, the population of Greater London grew from two million to six and a half million: it was the busiest metropolis in the world and had areas of great wealth to contrast with the many overcrowded and filthy slums. Arthur Conan Doyle, despite living in Hampshire when he wrote the first Sherlock Holmes stories, seems to have been drawn to the diversity and ambience of the city as a background for his novel. This extract shows London in the early morning when the city is 'already astir' and it could be considered a paradigm of how the author uses his background to enhance the atmosphere of the story.'

Theme Paragraph One: Conan Doyle's London can be interpreted as a metaphor for the complex and labyrinthine mysteries that Holmes investigates. Readers can feel pulled into the journey through the backstreets in the same way as they are pulled into the narrative of the investigation.

• Despite Holmes describing his methods of deduction

in the first chapter of the book as 'Simplicity itself', the adventure he and Watson embark upon, and its complicated and exotic Indian background, do not turn out to be straightforward. The twists and turns of the plot could be considered to be mirrored in this convoluted journey in the chapter 'The Episode of the Barrel'. The language Conan Doyle uses in this extract — 'parallel side-streets'; 'a curiously zig-zag road'; 'round in circles' — combined with the elongated sentences give the impression of a long and serpentine chase.[1] The reader might find it hard to keep up with the confusing trail left by Small and Tonga in the same way as it is hard to keep up with Holmes' racing mental processes; but, like the detective, the reader is on the scent of the answers to the plot's mysteries. [*AO1 for advancing the argument with a judiciously selected quote; AO2 for the close analysis of the language and for discussing how form and structure shape meaning*].

- Elsewhere in the novel: The chapter ends in bathos when Toby the dog is baffled by his catching the scent of a cask of creosote in a timber-yard. The way the dog 'stood upon the cask, looking from one to the other of us for some sign of appreciation' is an anthropomorphic expression which could remind the reader of the confusion of Athelney Jones, when he puts forward his erroneous theories to Holmes, hoping for approval.[2] There is an added comic touch in this passage when Conan Doyle writes: '"What the deuce is the matter with the dog?" growled Holmes'. The juxtaposition of 'dog' and 'growled' leads the reader to think of the animal making such a noise – that it is Holmes instead is an unexpected comedic device.

[AO1 for advancing the argument with a judiciously selected quote; AO2 for the close analysis of the language].

Theme Paragraph Two: In this extract and elsewhere in the novel, Conan Doyle uses the working population of London to set the scene and add human interest to Holmes' and Watson's journey.

- Not only the intricate cityscape of London, but also its citizens appear in this passage to give the background an authentically busy feel – to achieve the effect of daybreak bustle which gives the reader a sense of the early time of day as well as a view of the city scene. It is perhaps odd now to read that 'public-houses business was just beginning' and workers were having 'their morning wet' as this excerpt takes place just after sunrise, but for the majority of nineteenth century London, water was not safe to drink. After an epidemic of cholera mid-century, enormous effort was made to make drinking water cleaner, and by 1889 when *The Sign Of Four* was written, most (especially wealthier) areas had clean water, but in some poorer places it was still considered safer to drink beer, even for breakfast. *[AO1 for advancing the argument with a judiciously selected quote; AO3 for invoking relevant historical context].*
- The 'labourers and dockmen' are depicted as 'rough-looking' and the women busily 'taking down shutters and brushing doorsteps' are dismissed as 'slatternly' which seem rather elitist and condescending descriptions; but whether that is Watson's or the author's attitude, it is difficult to discern. *[AO1 for*

advancing the argument with a judiciously selected
quote; AO2 for the close analysis of the language].

- Elsewhere in the novel: Despite a certain patronising
attitude that Watson might have to blue-collar
workers, Conan Doyle arguably enjoys introducing
eccentric working-class Londoners into his novels. As
well as adding colour, Holmes' acquaintance with
unlikely characters such as the prizefighter McMurdo
at Pondicherry Lodge and Toby's owner the
menagerie collector Mr Sherman, shows the reader
that Holmes is an extraordinary man who has friends
and admirers in every walk of life. This adds to his
mystique, but at the same time could be said to show
that he is no elitist.

**Theme Paragraph Three: It can be argued that,
despite their surface knowledge, Conan Doyle's
descriptions of London lack detail and are often
superficial and unconvincing.**

- This passage contains many names of areas and
specific streets in London, which Watson names as he,
Holmes and the dog pass through them. It might be
thought that Conan Doyle was intimately
knowledgeable about these places and had possibly
'traversed' them himself. However, whereas Charles
Dickens used to walk for hours at night to become
fully conversant with the roads and boroughs of the
capital he minutely described in his novels, the same
is not the case for Conan Doyle. In fact Conan Doyle
was living in Southsea, 75 miles from London, when
he wrote *The Sign Of Four,* and had at that point in
time never lived in London ('I worked it all out from a

post office map', he told his publisher). [*AO3 for invoking relevant historical and literary context*].

- Certainly, while Conan Doyle uses a litany of place-names in this extract– 'Streatham, Brixton, Camberwell'; 'Bond Street and Miles Street' – he does not (beyond a nod to 'side-streets') hone in on details in the landscape that makes these areas unique, and this arguably exposes the superficiality of his knowledge. That said, the blurriness of the background – achieved through this mix of specificity of place-name and nonchalance towards on-the-ground details particular to those places – allows Holmes to remain overwhelmingly the chief character. [*AO1 for advancing the argument with a judiciously selected quote; AO2 for the close analysis of the language*].

- Elsewhere in the novel: In the previous chapter, Holmes asks Watson to '...go on to 3 Pinchin Lane, down near the water's edge at Lambeth'. It is an example of one of Conan Doyle's made-up places, since such a lane never existed. This might arguably be understood as a lack of interest in authenticity when it comes to the author's background to the action. So it is not surprising that the reader might feel as if the complicated journey taken by Holmes and Watson in this extract is more of a list of street names than a well-understood and genuine route. [*AO1 for advancing the argument with a judiciously selected quote*].

Conclusion

'It could be argued that by keeping the background far less specific and detailed than did other Victorian writers who set works in London, Conan Doyle created just the right amount of metropolitan atmosphere without letting the background overtake the heroes as the most interesting character. The descriptions of the cityscapes are lively and full of activity, but the author does not let them linger on too long or interrupt the suspense. In the Sherlock Holmes short story 'The Adventure Of The Empty House' Watson says 'Holmes' knowledge of the byways of London was extraordinary.' Possibly the same cannot be said of its author, but arguably he had just the right amount of knowledge to produce the effect he needed.'

Another drawing from Richard Gutschmidt: this one depicting Watson and Holmes following Toby!

At this point in the novel, Holmes decides he needs help to find Jonathan Small's boat, the "Aurora", so he has sent a telegram to The Baker Street Irregulars.

As he spoke, there came a swift pattering of naked feet upon the stairs, a clatter of high voices, and in rushed a dozen dirty and ragged little street-Arabs. There was some show of discipline among them, despite their tumultuous entry, for they instantly drew up in line and stood facing us with expectant faces. One of their number, taller and older than the others, stood forward with an air of lounging superiority which was very funny in such a disreputable little scarecrow.

"Got your message, sir," said he, "and brought 'em on sharp. Three bob and a tanner for tickets."

"Here you are," said Holmes, producing some silver. "In future they can report to you, Wiggins, and you to me. I cannot have the house invaded in this way. However, it is just as well that you should all hear the instructions. I want to find the where-abouts of a steam launch called the *Aurora*, owner Mordecai Smith, black with two red streaks, funnel black with a white band. She is down the river somewhere. I want one boy to be at Mordecai Smith's landing-stage opposite Millbank to say if the boat comes back. You must divide it out among yourselves, and do both banks thoroughly. Let me know the moment you have news. Is that all clear?"

"Yes, guv'nor," said Wiggins.

"The old scale of pay, and a guinea to the boy who finds the boat. Here's a day in advance. Now off you go!" He handed them a shilling each, and away they buzzed down the stairs, and I saw them a moment later streaming down the street.

"If the launch is above water they will find her," said Holmes, as he rose from the table and lit his pipe. "They can go every-where, see everything, overhear every one. I expect to hear before evening that they have spotted her.

Starting with this extract, discuss how Conan Doyle presents children in *The Sign of Four*.

Write about:

• How Conan Doyle presents children at this moment in the novel.

• **How Conan Doyle presents children in the novel as a whole.**

Introduction

'Conan Doyle does not include child characters of the middle or upper classes in the Holmes books, and his depictions of children are rare: they are limited to the 'Irregulars' and a few other youths of the working classes who are briefly involved in his adventures, sometimes to comic effect. So the way Conan Doyle depicts the life of 'Street arab' children in this extract and in the novel in general could be described as a limited and possibly parochial view of a particular class of child, although with this limitation in mind and the infrequent amount of mentions the children have in the canon, the impression they make is arguably a surprisingly memorable one.'[1]

Theme Paragraph One: Conan Doyle could be argued to portray poor children in *The Sign Of Four* as classic examples of homeless ragamuffins living on their wits in Victorian London; the 'Artful Dodger'' type as described by Charles Dickens.

- Fagin's gang of child thieves in Dickens' *Oliver Twist* was perhaps at least a partial inspiration for The Baker Street Irregulars, although Conan Doyle's group of youngsters appears to be on the opposite side of the law to The Artful Dodger and his confederates. Conan Doyle portrays these children similarly to Dickens' urchins in appearance, but we assume they all have homes to go to when necessary – they come by public transport to Baker Street at Holmes' behest and he pays their fares: 'Three bob and a tanner for tickets'. They do not seem to be runaways or juvenile criminals, simply boys who do not attend school (the school-leaving age was eleven or twelve for poorer pupils) and have not yet acquired adult jobs. [*AO1 for advancing the argument with a judiciously selected quote; AO3 for invoking relevant historical and literary context*].

- That the intelligence of these children is to be reckoned with can be inferred from the trust the cerebral Holmes places in them.[2] Holmes' instructions are meticulous and serious, and suggest in turn that he takes the children seriously: he tasks them with finding the boat, keeping watch ('one boy' must watch 'if the boat comes back', he insists), and ensuring the job is done 'thoroughly'.[3] Holmes' hyperbolic insinuation that the children will spot the boat so long as it has not sunk ('If the launch is above water they will find her') is a ringing endorsement of the boys' street-wise savvy. [*AO1 for advancing the argument with a judiciously selected quote; AO2 for the close analysis of the language*].

Theme Paragraph Two: The children might be considered as local "colour" rather than rounded characters; only one is given a name or differentiated from his companions.

- The repetitive assonance of 'pattering', 'clatter' and 'ragged' at the beginning of this excerpt leads the reader to feel the effect of the 'tumultuous entry' of the street children into the quiet gentlemen's residence of 221b Baker Street. As a crowd, they make a strong impression, but aside from Wiggins, their apparent leader, they are almost an amorphous group of interchangeable characters.[4] [*AO1 for advancing the argument with a judiciously selected quote; AO2 for the close analysis of the language*].

- Wiggins is described in almost affectionate terms as a 'disreputable little scarecrow', his 'air of lounging superiority...very funny' and as the other children receive no such descriptions, the reader arguably extrapolates that his companions share the same shabby and tattered appearance as their spokesman.[5] As scant attention is paid to individual characterisation, the Irregulars could be said to fulfil the role of background colour as much as the streets of London do throughout the story. [*AO1 for advancing the argument with a judiciously selected quote; AO2 for the close analysis of the language*].

- Elsewhere in the novel: Earlier in this chapter, when Holmes and Watson arrive at Mordecai Smith's boat hire business, there is a passage concerned with another child of a poor family – the boatman's six-year-old son. He is given the name Jack and merits a brief description – as 'curly-headed' – but he does not further the plot. He seems to be merely there to show how Holmes can 'strategically' use flattery to charm someone from whom he wishes to get information; in this case, the child's mother. Holmes' somewhat hollow praise: 'What a rosy-cheeked young rascal!'; 'A fine child, Mrs Smith!' shows that Holmes can from time to time be tactful, if it furthers his detective work. However, the interaction with the boy makes no impression on the plot narrative and can be viewed primarily as a moment of comic relief. [*AO1 for advancing the argument with a judiciously selected quote; AO2 for the close analysis of the language*].

Theme Paragraph Three: The Baker Street Irregulars can be thought of as almost a metaphor for Holmes himself; they are mavericks who work freelance and know London intimately.

- Just before this passage describing the invasion into their home by the Irregulars, Holmes tells Watson that the boys are 'The unofficial force'. This description could be equally applied to Holmes himself, the 'unofficial consulting detective' as he describes himself at the beginning of the first chapter of the novel, the echoing of the word 'unofficial' cementing the symmetry between them. He does appear to be doing the work of the official police force, but with far more skill and ability. [*AO1 for advancing the argument with a judiciously selected quote; AO2 for the close analysis of the language*].
- The way he deploys the children can be compared to the way Athelney Jones might use the constabulary, but Holmes knows that streetwise boys can explore London without raising the attention or the interest of local people, whereas policemen stand out and often people will draw their shutters and shut their mouths when they see the official force about. As the detective tells Watson, the children 'can go everywhere, see

everything, overhear everyone,' the tricolon sentence structure hammering home the sense of ubiquity the Irregulars are seemingly able to achieve.[6] *[AO1 for advancing the argument with a judiciously selected quote; AO2 for the close analysis of the language and for discussing how form and structure shape meaning].*

- They mirror Holmes himself in that they do not answer to anyone, they choose who they work for, they have no official capacity, yet they know their locale extremely well and will work tirelessly until they achieve their purpose.

Conclusion

'Conan Doyle's depiction of children in *The Sign Of Four* can be considered a limited one, since the reader sees nothing of the offspring of any class but the poorest, and only boys; no girls are mentioned. However, considering this rather narrow view of childhood, Conan Doyle manages to achieve a perhaps surprisingly powerful impact which has made his band of Baker Street Irregulars catch the public imagination in an extraordinary way. Conan Doyle portrays children as free-spirited junior intelligence agents who live lives utterly different from the way young people live today.'

A glass negative of Conan Doyle with his family: including, fittingly, his children!

ESSAY PLAN FIVE
READ THE FOLLOWING EXTRACT FROM
CHAPTER 10 OF THE SIGN OF FOUR AND
THEN ANSWER THE QUESTION THAT
FOLLOWS.

This extract is taken from a point in the novel when Holmes has found out the location of Jonathan Small's boat, and Holmes, Watson and Athelney Jones are having dinner before setting out to arrest Small.

Our meal was a merry one. Holmes could talk exceedingly well when he chose, and that night he did choose. He appeared to be in a state of nervous exaltation. I have never known him so brilliant. He spoke on a quick succession of subjects,—on miracle-plays, on mediæval pottery, on Stradivarius violins, on the Buddhism of Ceylon, and on the war-ships of the future,— handling each as though he had made a special study of it. His bright humour marked the reaction from his black depression of the preceding days. Athelney Jones proved to be a sociable soul in his hours of relaxation, and faced his dinner with the air of a *bon vivant*. For myself, I felt elated at the thought that we were nearing the end of our task, and I caught something of Holmes's gaiety. None of us alluded during dinner to the cause which had brought us together.

When the cloth was cleared, Holmes glanced at his watch, and filled up three glasses with port. "One bumper," said he, "to the success of our little expedition. And now it is high time we were off. Have you a pistol, Watson?"

"I have my old service-revolver in my desk."

"You had best take it, then. It is well to be prepared. I see that the cab is at the door. I ordered it for half-past six."

It was a little past seven before we reached the Westminster wharf, and found our launch awaiting us. Holmes eyed it critically.

"Is there anything to mark it as a police-boat?"

"Yes,—that green lamp at the side."

"Then take it off."

The small change was made, we stepped on board, and the ropes were cast off. Jones, Holmes, and I sat in the stern. There was one man at the rudder, one to tend the engines, and two burly police-inspectors forward.

Starting with this extract, explore how Conan Doyle presents Holmes as both an intellectual and a man of action in *The Sign of Four*.

Write about:

• **How Conan Doyle presents Holmes at this moment in the novel.**

• **How Conan Doyle presents Holmes in the novel as a whole.**

Introduction

Another good way to score AO3 (context) marks in an introduction is to demonstrate knowledge of other works in the Conan Doyle canon. Your knowledge does not need to be extensive – it simply needs to be relevant to the question at hand.

'In the first Holmes novel, *A Study In Scarlet*, his new flatmate John Watson outlines Holmes' specialised knowledge – or lack of it – and he concludes that while the detective's understanding of chemistry and sensational literature are 'profound', his knowledge of philosophy and serious literature are 'nil'. In this following story, Conan Doyle appears to be in the process of changing his hero's character and developing him into less of a specialist and more of a Renaissance Man, as this passage and other moments in *The Sign of Four* display. However, Holmes has always been portrayed as a man of action when he is on a case that seizes his interest, and both facets of his personality seem to be in play in this extract.'

Theme Paragraph One: This excerpt has Conan Doyle depicting Holmes as a sociable, talkative

**man – most unlike the Holmes Watson has hith-
erto described. His ability to talk on a wide variety
of subjects unconnected to detective work presents
Holmes as a man with great general knowledge.**

- The approaching climax of his case appears to have
  more effect on Sherlock Holmes than his seven-
  percent dose of cocaine produces – here he is in 'a
  state of nervous exaltation'. Watson has lived with him
  for several years by now and he 'ha[s] never known
  him so brilliant'. Readers have sometimes speculated
  on Holmes' mental health, and Watson mentions that
  this 'gaiety' comes after the detective's 'black
  depression in the preceding days' (due to a hiatus in
  the case described in the previous chapter 'A Break in
  the Chain'); giving an impression of a tendency
  towards wild mood swings.[1] Yet the detective himself
  shows his excitement and enthusiasm harmlessly, by
  taking various esoteric subjects and 'handling each as
  though he had made a special study of it'.[2] The
  subjects touch on music, religion and warfare – so
  again the reader sees the diversity of the hero's
  interests. [*AO1 for advancing the argument with a
  judiciously selected quote; AO2 for the close analysis
  of the language*].
- Elsewhere in the novel: At the beginning of the novel,
  before Mary Morstan visits Holmes, he remarks to
  Watson 'I cannot live without brainwork. What else is
  there to live for?'. There are many more allusions to
  his hyperactive mind, and several times when he
  quotes Goethe, La Rochefoucauld and other
  philosophers in their native tongues.[3] We know he
  can read these languages as well as speak them, since

Watson mentions Holmes receiving grateful letters
from a French detective 'with stray "magnifiques",
"coup de maitres" and "tours de force", all testifying to
the ardent admiration of the Frenchman'. The reader
is left in no doubt as to Holmes being a gifted polyglot
on top of all his other intellectual accompaniments.
[*AO1 for advancing the argument with a judiciously
selected quote; AO2 for the close analysis of the
language*].

**Theme Paragraph Two: The juxtaposition of
Holmes' informed and intellectual chat at dinner
with the immediate aftermath of potentially
deadly action emphasises the two distinct but
equally strong sides of Holmes' nature.**

- The focus in this extract is not just on Holmes-the-
  intellectual-raconteur, but on his ability to shapeshift
  between intellectual raconteur and man of action.[4]
  During the course of dinner, the very subject of taking
  action appears to have been exorcised – 'none of us
  alluded during dinner to the cause which had brought
  us together', Watson observes – and Holmes focuses
  solely on the cerebral.[5] [*AO1 for advancing the
  argument with a judiciously selected quote*].
- However, Holmes abruptly shifts gear midway
  through the extract, when he asks whether Watson
  has a gun: 'Have you a pistol, Watson?' That this
  query is abruptly tacked on to the end of paragraph
  functions to make it all the more surprising and
  abrupt. The effect, though jarring, emphasises how
  Holmes reconciles these two competing character-

traits within one persona: he is able to oscillate between the two at will. The narrative then quickly shifts to boarding the police boat – the speed of the transition mirroring Holmes' quickness to adapt – and Holmes, now man-of-action, takes charge in having the official green lamp removed: he seems equally at home and on top of the situation whether engaged in mental or physical effort. [*AO1 for advancing the argument with a judiciously selected quote; AO2 for discussing how form and structure shapes meaning*].

Theme Paragraph Three: Conan Doyle has Holmes performing actions of strength and agility in *The Sign of Four* which can be seen to contrast with the comparative physical weakness of most of the other characters.

- Rather remarkably, considering his drug use, Sherlock Holmes appears to be in extremely good physical health. When it is needed, he is the man of action that the situation demands. This extract does not directly allude to specific feats of athleticism, rather it displays the undoubted excitement and keenness that Holmes shows throughout the dinner in his eagerness to be in the midst of the action. He presents no fear, no doubt, no second thoughts, but only a desire to take the case it to its conclusion. Contrasted with the other major characters in the novel: the war-injured Watson, the 'stout, portly' Athelney Jones, the hypochondriac Thaddeus Sholto and the one-legged Jonathan Small, Sherlock Holmes is portrayed as a fine physical specimen. [*AO1 for advancing the argument with a judiciously selected quote*].

- <u>Elsewhere in the novel</u>: At the beginning of the chapter 'The Episode of The Barrel', Holmes' agility is called upon when he has to crawl upon the roof of Pondicherry lodge, following the route of Tonga the Andaman Islander. Watson describes the detective looking 'like an enormous glow-worm crawling along the ridge', after which he climbs down the long waterpipe and 'with a light spring he came on to the barrel, and from there to the earth' – indeed, the way in which this two-fold motion is effortlessly distilled into a single sentence mirrors Holmes' own effortlessness. His acrobatic skills are matched by his talent as a pugilist; when McMurdo the prizefighter recognises him, the reader hears that he and Holmes 'fought three rounds' and Holmes gave the seasoned boxer a 'cross-hit...under the jaw'.[6] It could be argued that these physical feats with which Conan Doyle endows his creation give him a sort of invulnerability, like a prototype of a modern superhero. [*AO1 for advancing the argument with a judiciously selected quote; AO2 for the close analysis of the language and for discussing how form shapes meaning*].

Conclusion

'This extract presents Holmes as a hero who is able to be a scintillating intellect and merry companion one moment, and a powerful man of action the next. As long as Holmes is in the throes of an interesting case, he appears to have infinite capabilities to transform himself into whatever the situation needs, whether literally, as when he disguises himself as an aged sailor, or metaphorically, when he can be a tough fighter or an inspiring conversationalist. 'My mind' he tells Watson at the start of the story, 'rebels at stagnation'. Judging by his inertia when unemployed, his body does too. Once on a case however, he appears able to do almost anything at all.'

Another statue of Sherlock Holmes — this one in Baker Street, London. Copyright © Nikos Roussos

At this point in the novel, the treasure box has just been recovered, and Watson has brought it to Mary Morstan.

"Is that the treasure, then?" she asked, coolly enough.

"Yes, this is the great Agra treasure. Half of it is yours and half is Thaddeus Sholto's. You will have a couple of hundred thousand each. Think of that! An annuity of ten thousand pounds. There will be few richer young ladies in England. Is it not glorious?"

I think that I must have been rather overacting my delight, and that she detected a hollow ring in my congratulations, for I saw her eyebrows rise a little, and she glanced at me curiously.

"If I have it," said she, "I owe it to you."

"No, no," I answered, "not to me, but to my friend Sherlock Holmes. With all the will in the world, I could never have followed up a clue which has taxed even his analytical genius. As it was, we very nearly lost it at the last moment."

"Pray sit down and tell me all about it, Dr. Watson," said she.

I narrated briefly what had occurred since I had seen her last,— Holmes's new method of search, the discovery of the *Aurora*, the appearance of Athelney Jones, our expedition in the evening, and the wild chase down the Thames. She listened with parted lips and shining eyes to my recital of our adventures. When I spoke of the dart which had so narrowly missed us, she turned so white that I feared that she was about to faint.

"It is nothing," she said, as I hastened to pour her out some water. "I am all right again. It was a shock to me to hear that I had placed my friends in such horrible peril."

"That is all over," I answered. "It was nothing. I will tell you no more gloomy details. Let us turn to something brighter. There is the treasure. What could be brighter than that? I got leave to bring it with me, thinking that it would interest you to be the first to see it."

"It would be of the greatest interest to me," she said. There was no eagerness in her voice, however.

Starting with this extract, discuss how Conan Doyle presents his characters' attitudes to the Great Agra Treasure in *The Sign of Four*.

Write about:

• **How Conan Doyle presents attitudes to the Great Agra Treasure at this moment in the novel.**

• **How Conan Doyle presents attitudes to the Great Agra Treasure in the novel as a whole.**

Introduction

- 'When Thaddeus Sholto, early in the novel, tells Mary Morstan, Holmes and Watson how much the Agra jewels are worth, Watson observes that: 'We all stared at one another open-eyed'. This is unsurprising, since the half a million pounds estimated value of the treasure is almost sixty million in today's money – an amazing sum, and enough to make Mary Morstan 'The richest heiress in England'. Yet as the narrative unfolds, the reader sees that attitudes to the treasure vary widely amongst the characters, dependent on how they see it affecting their lives. This extract describes the possible effect of the treasure on the romance of Watson and Mary Morstan, and intimates how its loss might be beneficial to their relationship.'

Theme Paragraph One: Mary Morston's attitude to the prospect of being the heiress to enormous wealth is unchanged throughout *The Sign of Four*. She is portrayed as the ideal of Victorian woman-hood, without avarice and unimpressed by the treasure even before the investigation begins.[1] Holmes is also an impartial party: his only

concern is the investigation and money does not interest him.

- Whereas we are given a direct line into Watson's thoughts via the first person narrative, we are not let into the secrets of Mary Morstan's heart. Her indifference to the Great Agra Treasure may be partly because she understands that John Watson will never seek to marry her if she becomes a very wealthy woman, but her lack of cupidity or wish for financial and social advancement is established from her first interview with Sherlock Holmes.[2] She seems to be a shining example of the most appreciated virtues of Victorian womanhood; her appearance is described as 'small, dainty...and dressed in the most perfect taste', with an expression 'sweet and amiable' while her eyes are 'spiritual and sympathetic'. We are looking through Watson's eyes, and it is a case of love at first sight; but also we might argue that many contemporary readers would find these 'womanly' characteristics exactly correspond with their idea of a perfect wife. She has even received valuable pearls as a gift, and despite being of 'limited means' she has not sold them, but is only interested in the mystery behind them, not their value. [*AO1 for advancing the argument with a judiciously selected quote; AO2 for the close analysis of the language; AO3 for invoking relevant historical context*].

- In this extract, Mary Morstan listens 'with parted lips and shining eyes' to Watson's relating of their capture of Jonathan Small. She feels so strongly that Watson 'feared she was about to faint' (fainting represented a female's acute sensitivity in contemporary literature), yet when discussing the treasure, she is unable to even appear keen: 'There was no eagerness in her voice, however'. [*AO1 for advancing the argument with a judiciously selected quote; AO3 for invoking literary-historical context*].

- <u>Elsewhere in the novel:</u> Sherlock Holmes also has an indifference to the treasure. As usual in his detective work, his only obsession is the solving of the case, and he barely mentions the jewels during the narrative. The policeman Athelney Jones, however, is very angry about the loss of the treasure because he and his constabulary would have received financial rewards had it been recovered. He considers it 'A very serious matter' and admonishes Jonathan Small for his deliberate action. [*AO1 for advancing the argument with a judiciously selected quote*].

Theme Paragraph Two: Conan Doyle presents Dr Watson as a romantic character who falls in love with Mary Morstan almost at first sight. His attitude to the treasure is that of hostility, because his sense of honour would forbid him courting a woman who was far richer than himself.

- The male fortune-hunter was a popular villain in Georgian and Victorian literature, from John Willoughby in Jane Austen's *Sense and Sensibility*, who abandons Marianne for a richer woman, to Jingle the eloper in Dickens' *The Pickwick Papers*. Women were often expected to help the family finances by marrying "well" – that is, to men better-off or of higher social position than themselves – whereas it was considered dishonourable for a man to eschew women of his own financial level to court a rich woman, and when married, live off her money.[3] [*AO3 for invoking relevant literary-historical context*].

- John Watson, being of a romantic, chivalric and modest nature, naturally adheres to that concept, and thus has to be 'overacting [his] delight' and has 'a hollow ring' in his congratulations, as he knows that when Mary is a rich woman, she is no longer within his reach as a wife. His happiness when the treasure is revealed to be lost, a few paragraphs later, is portrayed in a metaphor so fervent as to be almost ecstatic: '...I could realise nothing save that the golden barrier was gone from between us'. His proposal follows shortly afterwards, and at the end of the chapter they are engaged — the structural choice of clumping these developments within a single chapter adding emphasis. [*AO1 for advancing the argument with a judiciously selected quote; AO2 for the close analysis of the language and for discussing how structure shapes meaning*].

Theme Paragraph Three: The attitudes of Watson and Morstan in this extract are unusual in the context of *The Sign of Four*, where fascination with, and desire for, the treasure cause a violent and tragic chain of events. The treasure has an almost mythical importance in the eyes of Jonathan Small.

- When Jonathan Small first hears about the treasure, as he relates in his confessional narrative in the chapter following this passage, his first thought are 'what [he] might do in the old country with it...' In his wild dreams of returning home with pockets full of gold he sees himself as having some sort of revenge on people who had thought of him as a 'ne'er do well' when he was a young man. The reader can see that ideas of revenge become as important to him as his wish for the treasure. The contrast between the extract above, where two people are made far happier by losing the fortune than by owning it, and the exultant cry by Small – 'It is my treasure, and if I can't have the loot I'll take darned good care that no one else does' – invites the reader to examine the disparate attitudes; Small has unwittingly done Watson and Mary Morstan a very good turn in consigning the treasure to the bottom of the Thames. [*AO1 for advancing the argument with a judiciously selected quote; AO2 for the close analysis of the language*].

- The Great Agra Treasure turns out to be the death of many who love it too dearly or stand in the way of those who do: John Morstan, Bartholomew Sholto, Achmet the hapless merchant, the Pathan convict guard and Tonga the Andaman Islander all die for reasons connected with the jewels that Small lovingly describes in great detail after his arrest: 'one hundred and forty-three diamonds...including The Great Mogul...ninety-seven very fine emeralds...' He names many other stones and can recall each one with the memory of an obsessive fantasist. [*AO1 for advancing the argument with a judiciously selected*].

- Another sign of his fanatical determination to either regain the treasure or kill the man who took it, is his ability to wait, nurturing his greed and hatred until he is ready to strike. He and Tonga had been back in England for three or four years before Small decided the time was right to steal back the treasure, and then they struck only because they heard that Major Sholto was dying. By this time the treasure was a true obsession to Small, although becoming a secondary one; as he himself said, he 'lived only for vengeance... Even the Agra treasure had come to be a smaller thing in my mind than the slaying of Sholto'. [*AO1 for advancing the argument with a judiciously selected quote*].

Conclusion

'The avaricious desire for The Great Agra Treasure causes misery to those who want it so much that they lose their moral compass. Violence, obsession and revenge follow upon covetousness. Jonathan Small says that as soon as he thought about the treasure, 'Whether Achmet, the merchant, lived or died was a thing as light as air to me'. This passage, where John Watson and Mary Morstan come together blissfully because they have *lost* the treasure, is a joyful counterpoint to the novel's tragedies. Conan Doyle, it can be argued, is making the moral argument that extreme wealth does not bring happiness, but instead the timeless virtues of moderation, honesty, and above all love should be prioritised.'

Cover art for a graphic novel version of a
Holmesian quest!

At this point in the novel, Jonathan Small has been captured, and is being questioned about the recent events by Holmes and Athelney Jones.

"Justice!" snarled the ex-convict. "A pretty justice! Whose loot is this, if it is not ours? Where is the justice that I should give it up to those who have never earned it? Look how I have earned it! Twenty long years in that fever-ridden swamp, all day at work under the mangrove-tree, all night chained up in the filthy convict-huts, bitten by mosquitoes, racked with ague, bullied by every cursed black-faced policeman who loved to take it out of a white man. That was how I earned the Agra treasure; and you talk to me of justice because I cannot bear to feel that I have paid this price only that another may enjoy it! I would rather swing a score of times, or have one of Tonga's darts in my hide, than live in a convict's cell and feel that another man is at his ease in a palace with the money that should be mine." Small had dropped his mask of stoicism, and all this came out in a wild whirl of words, while his eyes blazed, and the handcuffs clanked together with the impassioned movement of his hands. I could understand, as I saw the fury and the passion of the man, that it was no groundless or unnatural terror which had possessed Major Sholto when he first learned that the injured convict was upon his track.

"You forget that we know nothing of all this," said Holmes quietly. "We have not heard your story, and we cannot tell how far justice may originally have been on your side."

"Well, sir, you have been very fair-spoken to me, though I can see that I have you to thank that I have these bracelets upon my wrists. Still, I bear no grudge for that. It is all fair and above-board. If you want to hear my story I have no wish to hold it back. What I say to you is God's truth, every word of it. Thank you; you can put the glass beside me here, and I'll put my lips to it if I am dry.

Starting with this extract, explain how far you think Conan Doyle portrays Jonathan Small as a sympathetic character in _The Sign of Four_.

Write about:

• How far Conan Doyle portrays Jonathan Small as sympathetic at this moment in the novel.

• How far Conan Doyle portrays Jonathan Small as sympathetic in the novel as a whole.

Introduction

'There are arguably several hints in this extract, and in *The Sign of Four* as a whole, that the author does not wish the antagonist of the story, the criminal Jonathan Small, to be considered a wholly wicked man. By giving Small the chance to tell his story and exculpate himself if he can, the reader can identify with Holmes in reserving judgement until all the facts – at least from Small's point of view – have come out; like the detective '...we cannot tell how far justice may have been on [his] side'. This extract comes directly after Athelney Jones has reprimanded Small for throwing the jewels into the river, and is Small's response to being told he had thwarted justice.'

Theme Paragraph One: Conan Doyle devotes the last, and longest, chapter of *The Sign of Four* to Jonathan Small's personal story, and this passage from it shows Small to be a man who feels life has treated him badly, but finally accepts his fate and is prepared to be honest about what he has done.

- By giving Small a whole chapter to narrate the story of his life — a stark structural choice — we may believe that the author wishes the reader to see that although the nature with which a man is born may play a large part in his life choices (and the young Jonathan Small admits some bad decisions and is clearly of a vengeful and passionate temperament), the cruelty and suffering he undergoes in life can turn him from merely a headstrong man into a bitter, angry person who feels that he is entitled to be compensated for his sufferings. The powerful words Small uses in this extract to describe what he went through: 'chained up...filthy convict-huts...bitten by mosquitoes...racked with ague...bullied...' add up to an appalling experience, especially perhaps for a man with a disability. The reader arguably feels pity and understanding at this point, even though we know some of the criminal's misdeeds. [*AO1 for advancing the argument with a judiciously selected quote; AO2 for the close analysis of the language and for discussing how structure shapes meaning*].

• Elsewhere in the novel: Small himself, although admitting to the crimes he did commit, is still convinced at the end that he is more of a victim than his own victims are. After his story is finished, he forcefully reiterates his sense of grievance: 'how badly I have myself been served by Major Sholto, and how innocent I am of the death of his son'. The delusion that he is innocent, when he was the one who brought Tonga into Pondicherry Lodge, not to mention the premise that he was entitled to take vengeance into his own hands, might mitigate any pity that the reader has been feeling thus far. [*AO1 for advancing the argument with a judiciously selected quotee*].

Theme Paragraph Two: Throughout the novel, although Small is complicit in other crimes, the only man he actually kills is a prison guard who he

**claims had tormented him over many years, and
he shows regret for other deaths.**

- Despite his debatable culpability in other crimes, it is
quite clear that to deliberately unstrap his wooden leg
and 'knock the whole front' of a man's head in with it,
is a violent murder by Small. Revenge for past
humiliations by the Pathan guard seems reason
enough to him, although that is how he and Tonga
manage to escape from prison. In this passage, Small
claims 'What I say to you is God's truth, every word of
it' and he does seem to hold none of his crimes back
from the detectives. Yet arguably he considers this one
deliberate killing justifiable, as he mentions no qualms
about it, unlike when he is instrumental in the death
of Achmet, and has momentary pity for the innocent
merchant. But he 'only' trips Achmet, enabling his
murder rather than committing it; a difference he
seems to feel is important, although the reader may
think otherwise. [*AO1 for advancing the argument
with a judiciously selected quote; AO2 for the close
analysis of the language*].

- Small also frightens Major Sholto to death – though it
could arguably have been the Major's guilty
conscience (rather than the fear of the man he robbed)
which caused his heart to fail. Bartholomew Sholto's
death is later blamed solely on Tonga the Indaman
Islander, and Small claims to have been angry at the
murder – 'I had no part in it, sir', as it was only
Bartholomew's father he blamed, not his son. Yet
despite pity for his circumstances, it is hard to find
Small blameless in any of these deaths – especially
when in this excerpt he seems to think the ends

justified the means, and the treasure should still be his: 'Look how I have earned it!' [*AO1 for advancing the argument with a judiciously selected quote; AO2 for the close analysis of the language*].

Theme Paragraph Three: Many of the characters and events in *The Sign of Four* show treachery and racism, but Small is not always portrayed as racist or disloyal by Conan Doyle, and he cared for Tonga, the Andaman Islander, when he was very ill.

- In this extract, Jonathan Small is impassioned, with eyes blazing, as the author alliteratively portrays him 'in a wild whirl of words'. He refers angrily to 'every cursed black-faced policeman who loved to take it out of a white man'. Yet, although Small sometimes speaks with typical contemporary racist attitudes, he is by no means a confirmed racist by nature, and in *The Sign Of Four* there are many times where he is loyal to his Sikh co-thieves Abdullah Khan, Mahomet Singh and Dost Akbah. When the treacherous Major Sholto asks him 'What have three black fellows to do with our agreement?' Small could have easily left them out of it, but instead he responds 'Black or blue, they are in with me, and we all go together.' Indeed the very title of the book, *The Sign of* [*the*] *Four,* refers to the messages Small leaves to his victims, showing that he has not forgotten the original pact between them. In this passage he asks 'Whose loot is this, if it is not *ours*?', not 'mine' but 'ours' – even at this late point he is still steadfast to their agreement.

[AO1 for advancing the argument with a judiciously selected quote; AO2 for the close analysis of the language].

- <u>Elsewhere in the novel</u>: Interestingly, the descriptions of Tonga from Watson, when he and Holmes are chasing Small's boat along the river, as a 'savage, distorted creature' with features 'deeply marked with all bestiality and cruelty' are very different to Small's friendly, even loving remarks about the Islander. Tonga had been abandoned by his own tribe as he was ill and dying, yet Small cared for him and devoted time and effort to his recovery, depicting him as 'staunch and true...no man ever had a more faithful mate'. *[AO1 for advancing the argument with a judiciously selected quote; AO2 for the close analysis of the language].*

- Admittedly, when back in England Small exhibits the Islander at fairs, for money, but that was not considered unusual behaviour at the time, and by Small's account Tonga co-operated of his own will, eating raw meat and dancing 'his war-dance' for their livelihood. By contemporary Victorian standards, Tonga seems to have been treated well by his friend. However, Small shows no particular sadness at Tonga's death; most of his pity appears to be kept for himself. *[AO1 for advancing the argument with a judiciously selected quote; AO3 for invoking literary context].*

Conclusion

'Early in the novel, Holmes asks Watson 'Are you well up in your Jean Paul?' This reference to the German philosopher Jean Paul Richter is particularly prescient here, since a famous quotation of Richter's refers to his belief that 'The conscience of children is formed by the influences that surround them; their notions of good and evil are the result of the moral atmosphere they breathe'. By giving Jonathan Small the back story he does, Conan Doyle could be understood to wish the reader to have a degree of sympathy for this criminal who has some appealing characteristics to set against the clearly destructive personality traits which have got him to prison, if not the gallows.'

Conan Doyle's grave in Minstead, Hampshire.

ENDNOTES

ESSAY PLAN ONE

1. The Romantic era loosely refers to the period of time between the French Revolution (1789) and William IV's ascension to the throne in 1830. The Romantic poets were obsessed with nature and powerful emotions.
   Empiricism refers to a philosophy that prioritises evidence above all else.
2. The word dichotomy refers to when you have two contrasting things.
   If two things are converging, it means that they are coming together or overlapping.
3. To remonstrate is to forcefully protest.
4. An author breaks the fourth wall when they draw attention to the fictionality of their own work.
5. To be brusque is to be blunt to a degree that borders on rudeness.
6. To be piqued by something is to be resentful of it.

ESSAY PLAN TWO

1. If something is unaesthetic, it means it is ugly or unattractive.
2. Hyperbole means something very similar to exaggeration.
3. To affect means to pretend.

ESSAY PLAN THREE

1. The word serpentine means snake-like.
2. To anthropomorphise a non-human entity is to give this non-human entity human-like characteristics.

ESSAY PLAN FOUR

1. To have a parochial outlook is to have narrow outlook based on a limited frame of reference.
2. To be cerebral means to be intelligent!
3. To be meticulous is to do things with rigorous care and attention to detail.
4. To be amorphous is to lack a clear shape or definition.

5. To extrapolate is to conclude on the basis of what evidence you have available.
6. Tricolon – also known as 'the rule of three' – is when you have three items, things or words clumped together.

ESSAY PLAN FIVE

1. A hiatus is a break or a gap of time.
2. If something is esoteric it means it is obscure.
3. An allusion is a reference.
4. A raconteur is a story-teller/skilled conversationalist.
5. If you have exorcised something, it means you have gotten rid or dispelled it.
6. A pugilist is a boxer.

ESSAY PLAN SIX

1. Avarice means something akin to greed.
2. Cupidity again means something similar to greed.
3. To eschew something means to reject it.

ACCOLADE PRESS FOR GCSE ENGLISH: THE RANGE

www.accoladetuition.com/accolade-gcse-guides

ENGLISH LITERATURE

Romeo and Juliet: Essay Writing Guide for GCSE (9-1)

Macbeth: Essay Writing Guide for GCSE (9-1)

Power and Conflict: Essay Writing Guide for GCSE (9-1)

Dr Jekyll and Mr Hyde: Essay Writing Guide for GCSE (9-1)

A Christmas Carol: Essay Writing Guide for GCSE (9-1)

The Merchant of Venice: Essay Writing Guide for GCSE (9-1)

Love and Relationships: Essay Writing Guide for GCSE (9-1)

Great Expectations: Essay Writing Guide for GCSE (9-1)

An Inspector Calls: Essay Writing Guide for GCSE (9-1)

Pride and Prejudice: Essay Writing Guide for GCSE (9-1)

Unseen Poetry: Essay Writing Guide for GCSE (9-1)

Lord of the Flies: Essay Writing Guide for GCSE (9-1)

Much Ado About Nothing: Essay Writing Guide for GCSE (9-1)

ENGLISH LANGUAGE

English Language Paper One: A Technique Guide for GCSE (9-1)

English Language Paper Two : A Technique Guide for GCSE (9-1)

If you found this book useful, please consider leaving a review on Amazon.

You can also join our private Facebook group (where our authors share resources and guidance) by visiting the following link: **https://rcl.ink/DME.**